EYE BOGGLERS

EYE BOGGLERS

A Mesmerizing Mass of Amazing Illusions

CARLTON KIDS

Gianni A. Sarcone
and **Marie-Jo Waeber**

This is a Carlton book

Text and artwork copyright
© 2011 Archimedes' Laboratory Ltd
Design copyright © 2011 Carlton Books Limited

Executive Editor: Barry Timms
Project Editor: Lara Maiklem
Senior Art Editor: Jake da'Costa
Designer: Joanne Mitchell
Cover Design: Jake da'Costa
Creative Director: Clare Baggaley
Production: Kate Pimm

This paperback edition published in 2011 by Carlton Books Limited
An imprint of the Carlton Publishing Group
20 Mortimer Street, London W1T 3JW

First published in 2011 by Carlton Books Limited

2 4 6 8 10 9 7 5 3 1

A catalogue record for this book is
available from the British Library.

ISBN: 978-1-78097-074-5
Printed in Dongguan, China

GET READY...

Your eyes – those incredible jelly balls beneath your forehead – capture everything around you. They are sense organs allowing you to see, and they give more information about your surroundings than any of the other four senses: hearing, taste, touch and smell.

But what you see also depends on your brain. It receives electrical signals from the eyes and uses these to make sense of what is seen. But the brain also adds two extra ingredients of its own: memory and meaning.

It is because of these extra two things that the brain is sometimes tricked by the eyes. When you see something that is not really there, or something different from what is really there, you are experiencing an optical illusion.

This book is intended to surprise and entertain, and also to encourage you, dear reader, to always look beyond what you see... Have fun!

Gianni A. Sarcone and Marie-Jo Waeber
Researchers and artists

Dotty Circles

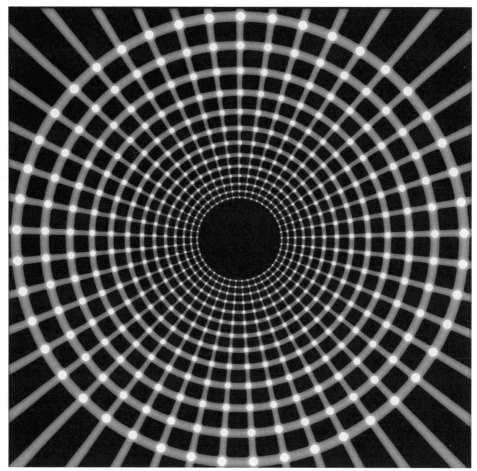

Scan your eyes across these circles. Can you see little brown dots start to appear and disappear all over the pattern?

The Impossible Vault

Does this door open outwards or inwards? Your money wouldn't be very safe in here!

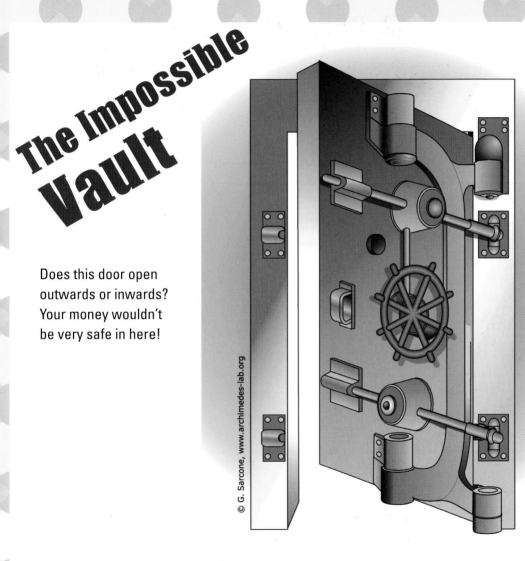

© G. Sarcone, www.archimedes-lab.org

Arrow Arrow

How many arrows can you see? Are you sure? Count them again...
(Answer on page 94)

Ant Army

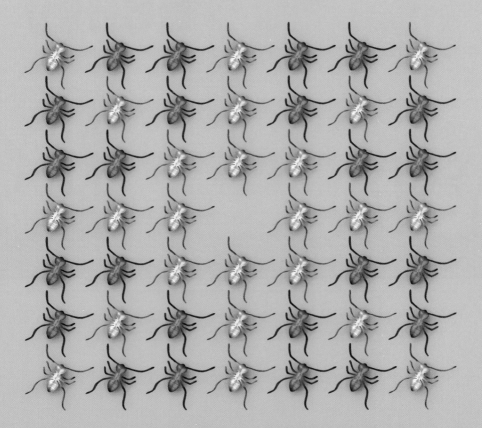

Without counting them, are there more red ants or white ants?
(Answer on page 94)

Light or Heavy

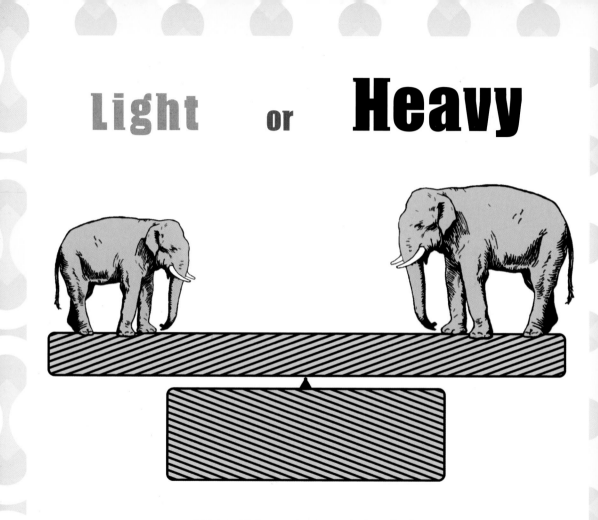

Which of these elephants is heavier?
(Answer on page 94)

Crazy Wavy

The lines in this picture might look wavy…

But are they? (Answer on page 94)

Famous Face

Start by looking at this picture close up. Slowly move the book away from you until a face appears. Who is it? (Answer on page 94)

Spaghetti Twist

©1996 [signature]

Does the hanging, striped spaghetti bulge inwards or outwards?
(Answer on page 94)

Up the Garden Path

Follow the paths… Which is the longest: A to B or A to C?

(Answer on page 94)

Van Cram

Can you fit all these boxes into the van?
Try tracing the boxes onto a piece of
paper, cut them out and see if you can
make them fit. (Answer on page 94)

Hidden in the Petals

Can you find an animal hidden in this rose?
(Answer on page 94)

All Alone?

Is this old lady really alone? How many people can you see with her?

Face of Fruits

The artist who painted this clever portrait using fruit and vegetables also painted people made of books, flowers and even fish!

Towering
Temples

Which of the temples is taller, A or B?
(Answer on page 94)

Shhh, Someone's Listening!

The man reading the book appears to be on his own, but is he?
Can you see who's with him?

Could you bathe at this beach?
Follow the shoreline and see…

Above

or Below?

Notice anything strange? The way this structure is drawn means
you can look up at one man, while looking down at the other!

Dog or Cat?

Hidden in this picture is a very ugly dog and a cute cat.
Can you find them both? (Answer on page 94)

Sea Legs

At first glance this might seem like a normal line of sailors, but look carefully...
Can you see something strange going on with their legs?

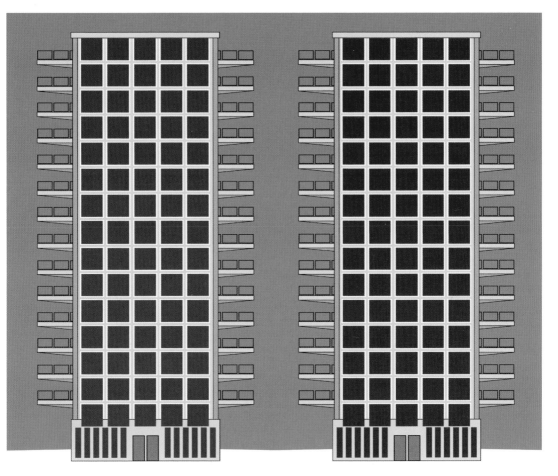

Spot the Spots

Glance across these buildings. Can you see grey dots appearing and vanishing where the window frames meet each other?

Golden Dome

Which two colours make up the golden dome on this building? Look carefully, you may be surprised!

(Answer on page 94)

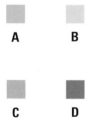

A   B

C   D

Stripe Selection

Can you tell which bar (A or B) matches the bar in the red and green box?
(Answer on page 94)

A

B

Bendy Legs

Look very carefully, are the legs of these funny-looking men straight or bent?

(Answer on page 94)

Arrow

Fourth

Trace these arrows onto a piece of paper. Cut them out, cut each one in half, then rearrange the pieces to make a fourth arrow. (Answer on page 94)

Going Up!

Whatever direction these men are facing they always seem to be going up. How will they ever get down!

Tilting Squares

©98, G. Sarcone. www.archimedes-lab.org

These squares look as if they are tilting to the left when they are actually perfectly upright.

A Foxy Puzzle

There are more animals than you think in this picture. See if you can find
a boar, a horse and a lamb hidden in the undergrowth.
(Answer on page 94)

The Floating Vase

The Floating Vase

What do you see? A shadow under a floating vase
or just a stain on the tablecloth.

If you move your eyes round and round this clock the cogs will start to look as if they are moving.

Cat or Mouse ?

This cat is looking for a mouse. Can you find it?

Shrinking

Relax and look at the centre of this picture. You should start to see the purple discs move towards the centre of the circle.

expanding

Do the same with this picture,
but this time the green discs should
start to move away from the centre.
Remember to stay relaxed!

Hidden Baby

Can you help the mother panda find her baby?
(Answer on page 94)

Lonely Dancers

These dancers are having fun, but are they really alone?
(Answer on page 94)

Carpet Capers

A

B

These two women are in a race to see who will finish the cleaning first. Who do you think has the shortest length of carpet to vacuum – A or B? (Answer on page 94)

Where You Bean?

Can you find a child's face hiding in these coffee beans? (Answer on page 94)

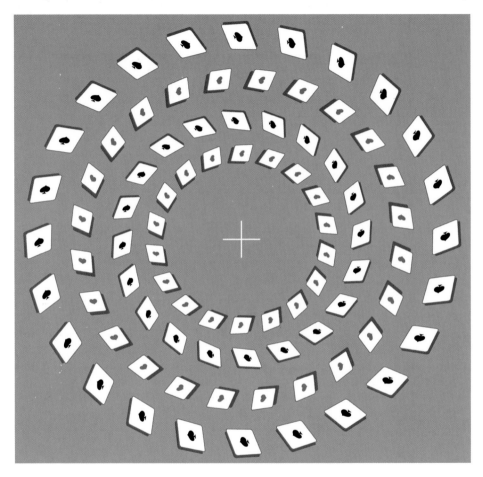

Circling Cards

Focus on the cross in the middle and move the book towards and away from you. Do you notice anything strange?

Hovering Helicopters

Look carefully at both of these helicopters.
Which line is longer: blue or red?
(Answer on page 94)

Tall
and
Small

Which of these men is
the tallest? Mind you
don't get caught out!
(Answer on page 94)

Shooting Stars

Relax and concentrate on this picture. The stars should start
to pulsate and the white background should turn slightly blue.

How Many Angels?

How many angels can you see in this picture?
(Answer on page 95)

Jiggling Jellyfish

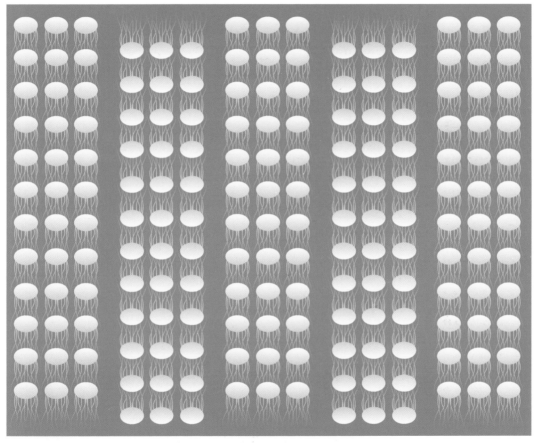

Imagine you are looking at a sea of jellyfish. Stare at the picture then move your eyes around the groups and the jellyfish will start to move.

Spooky Face

Stare at this picture until a rather spooky hidden face starts to appear.

Bear or Seal?

Is this a bear crawling out of a hole in the ice or a seal enjoying a rest?

Black or **White**

Is this a white wall being painted black or a black wall being painted white?

Chicks in the Nest

Can you find ten birds within this picture?
(Answer on page 95)

The Perfect Circle?

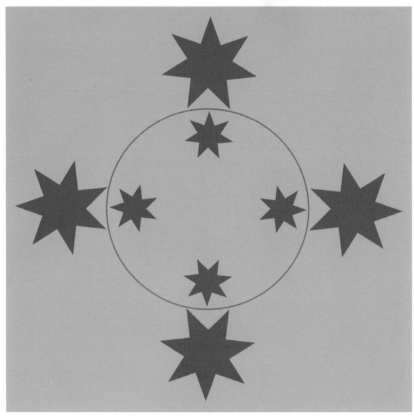

Is this circle perfectly round?

(Answer on page 95)

Faces

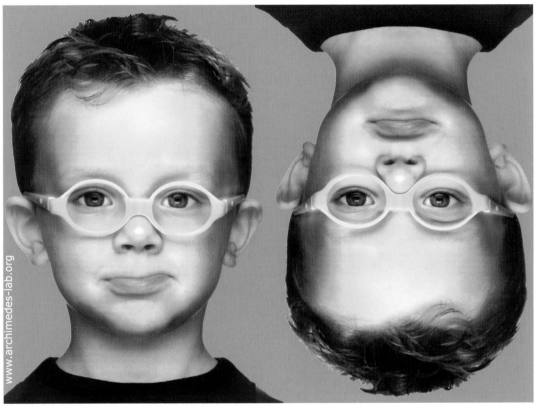

Faces

Without turning the book upside down, find two differences between these boys.
When you've given up you can turn the book around!

A Very Odd Place

There are five crazy things going on in this picture, can you find them all?
(Answer on page 95)

Crazy Car

Do you think you could drive this vehicle?

Towering Man

This man looks taller that the Eiffel Tower, but he is larger because he is closer to the camera. These sort of pictures are easy to set up, so why not try it with your own camera?

Impossible Stairs

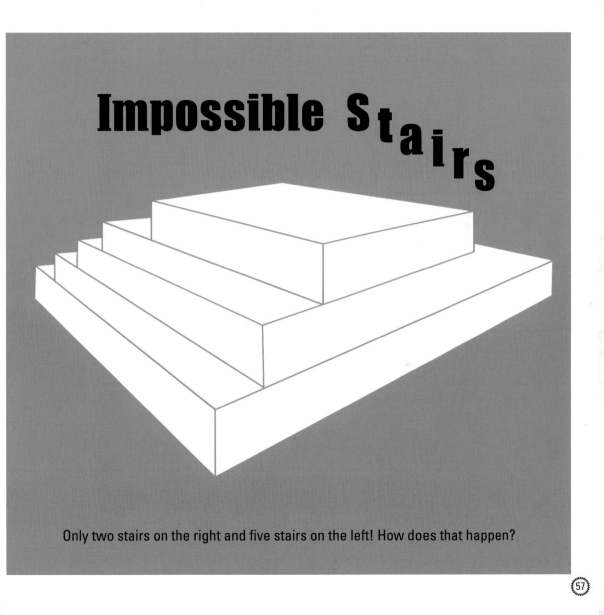

Only two stairs on the right and five stairs on the left! How does that happen?

Lady in the Landscape

A sailing boat through some trees on a dark night, or a woman's face?
(Clue: the boat is her nose and mouth.)

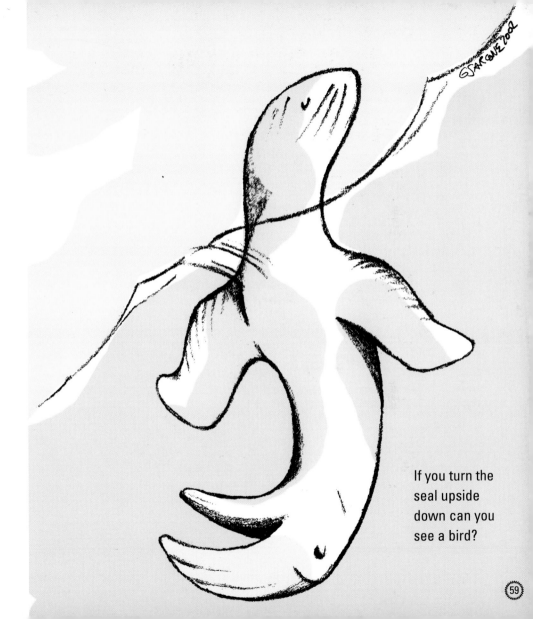

Seal Shapes

If you turn the
seal upside
down can you
see a bird?

Tiger Tiger

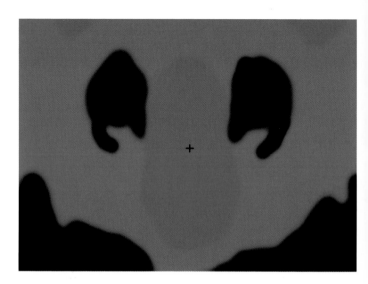

Stare at the cross
in the blue picture
for 15 seconds,
then quickly stare
at the cross in
the tiger picture.
What happens?
(Answer on page 95)

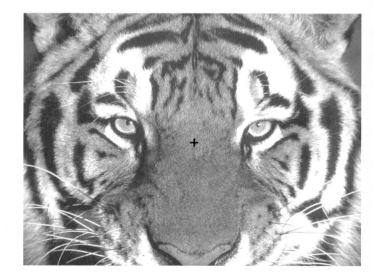

Hidden
Faces

Can you see the faces outlined by the sides of these cups? They are frowning, sticking their tongues out and laughing at each other!

Keep on Climbing

Could you get to the top of these stairs?

Rotating Rings

Focus on the cross in the middle of the circle then move the book away from you and towards you. Be careful, it could make you dizzy!

A World of Hair

Hidden in this map of the world is the face of a girl with lots of hair. Can you see her?

All Tied Up

Which line of coloured
squares is most like the line
that runs down the middle of the tie?
(Answer on page 95)

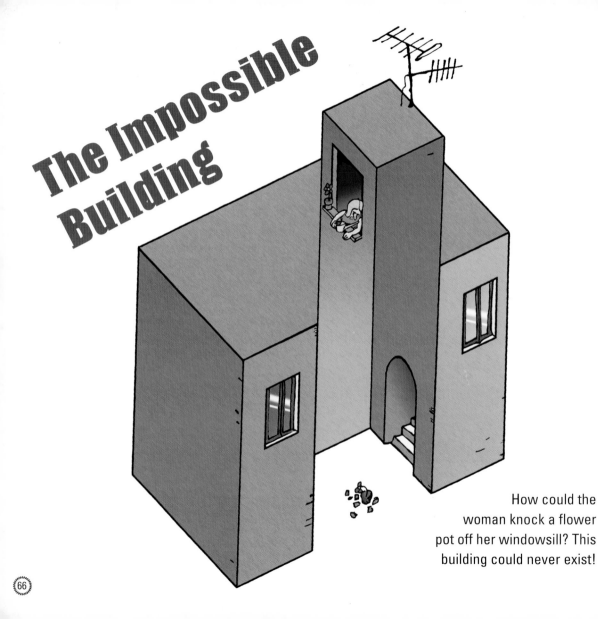

The Impossible Building

How could the woman knock a flower pot off her windowsill? This building could never exist!

Box Clever

Give the boxers a ring! Draw a square that connects all eight dots. (Answer on page 95)

The Magic Glass

Can you take one of these glasses off the tray?

(Answer on page 95)

Crawling Creepers

Stare at these slithery snakes for while before moving your gaze around the picture. The snakes will look as if they are wriggling on the page.

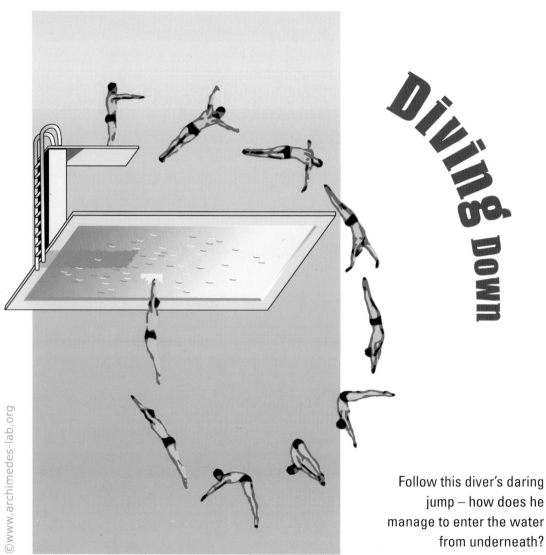

Diving Down

Follow this diver's daring jump – how does he manage to enter the water from underneath?

Phantom Tomato

Is this a tomato on a plate or just the stalk on an empty plate? Count the prongs on the fork, how many does it have? Are you sure?

Under the Arches

These arches don't look quite right.
Can you see what is wrong with them?

Twisted Chair

Are you looking at
this chair from behind
or from the front?
Are you sure?

Hypnotic Halos!

Don't stare at this one for too long or it might hypnotize you!

What Is It?

Can you guess what this picture is? There is no right or wrong answer and your guess might even be funnier than our suggestion. (Answer on page 95)

Off-Colour Cow

The colour in this picture is not balanced. Can you see that there is more blue on one side and more yellow on the other? To balance the colour, stare at the fly in the second picture for 30 seconds, then look at the cow again.

Guess the Picture

Have a guess at what this picture might be. There is no wrong or right answer,
so let your imagination run wild! (Answer on page 95)

Animal Magic

Can you see a second zebra hidden in the stripes of the main one?

Trace these shapes onto a piece of paper and cut them out. Now try to assemble them into the shape of a cross. It's not as easy as you think! (Answer on page 95)

Spiral Snail

The shell of this snail looks like one big spiral ... but is it?
Look again and you will see that it is actually made
up of lots of circles, each inside the other.

Hide and Seek

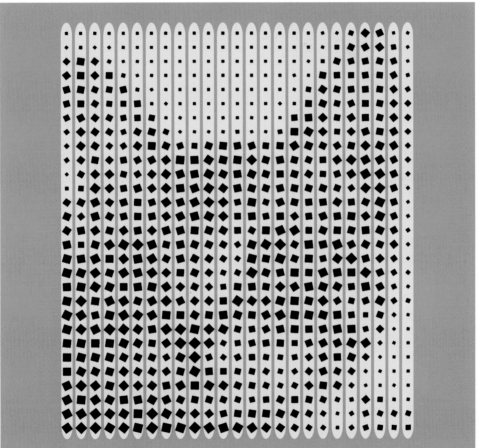

Prop the book up with this page open and walk away from it. As you
get further away from it can you see something start to appear?

Which of these bowling balls is larger.
Remember, this is a book of optical
illusions so think carefully!
(Answer on page 95)

Bowling Balls

The Cheshire Cat

Can you see a cat in the middle of the blue area? To make it disappear, close one eye and stare at the blue area for 15–20 seconds. If you keep staring the cat will reappear.

Lively Leprechaun

1 2 3 4 5 6

Hold this page about 30 cm in front of you and close your right eye. Focus on a number at a time, starting with 1, and count up slowly. By the time you reach 4, the leprechaun will have disappeared.

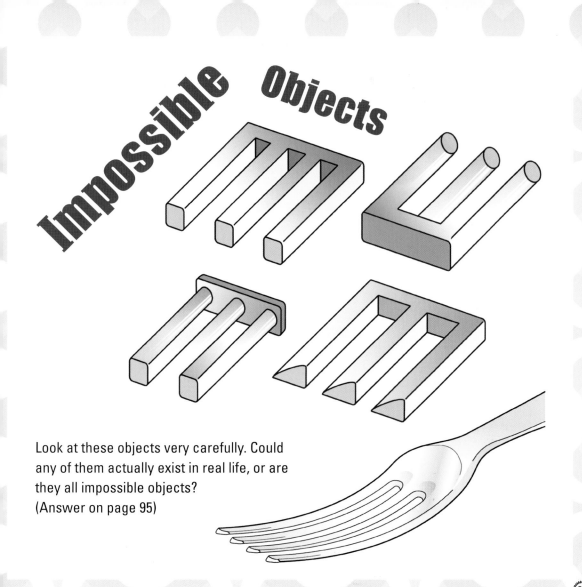

Impossible Objects

Look at these objects very carefully. Could any of them actually exist in real life, or are they all impossible objects?
(Answer on page 95)

Happy

At first glance these look like two normal dogs, but look again and you'll see they are a bit muddled up!

Dogs

Wild Child

Can you spot the face of a boy hidden in the tiger's fur?
(Answer on page 95)

Fairer Pharaoh

Can you crack this Egyptian boggler? Which of the statues
seems darker? (Answer on page 95)

Magic Wardrobe

Without measuring them, which green line looks longer: A–B or C–D?
(Answer on page 95)

Tricky Triangles

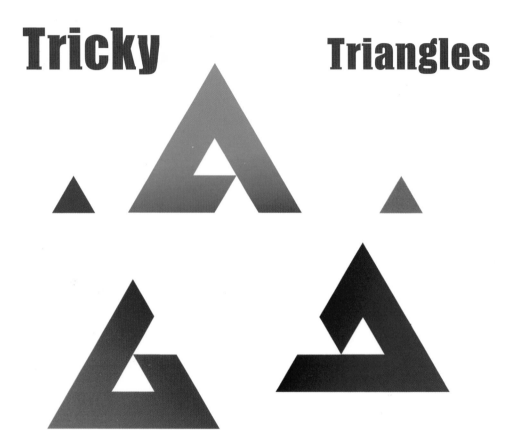

How many triangles can you count here? Look very carefully, there are more than you think.
(Answer on page 95)

Bright Bulb

Is the yellow circle in the middle of this picture darker than its surround? What happens when you move it closer and further away from you? (Answer on page 95)

Waiting and watching

Can you see a face watching this rower? Here's a clue: look under the bridge.

Leaning Tower Paintings

Crooked pictures can be very annoying. Can you make out which picture
of the Leaning Tower of Pisa in Italy is not hanging straight?

(Answer on page 95)

Answers

p.8 Arrows
There are eight arrows altogether, did you find them all?

p.9 Ant Army
You probably thought there were more white ants, but there are actually equal numbers of red and white ants.

p.10 Light or Heavy
The answer is neither! It's an optical illusion and the balance is perfectly level.

p.11 Crazy Wavy
If you check each line with a ruler you will find that they are all straight.

p.12 Famous Face
Did you find the famous painting of the Mona Lisa?

p.13 Spaghetti Twist
All the lines are straight and none of them bulge in any way.

p.14 Up the Garden Path
If you measure them with a ruler you will find they are the same length.

p.15 Van Cram
All the boxes will fit in the van.

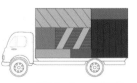

p.16 Hidden in the Petals
It's a dolphin, did you find it?

p.17 All Alone?
Look carefully at the shape created by each cat's tail and back leg and you will see the faces of five people.

p.19 Towering Temples
Both temples A and B are the same height.

p.20 Shh, Someone's Listening!
Turn the book around and you will be able to see a face in the mountains behind the man.

p.23 Dog or Cat?
To find the cat turn the page upside down.

p.26 Golden Dome
Would you believe the answer is C and D!

p.27 Stripe Selection
The bar is actually the same colour all the way along, so the answer is A.

p.28 Bendy Legs
They are straight! It is the lines in the circles that make them appear bent.

p.29 Fourth Arrow
Did you get it right?

p.32 A Foxy Puzzle
The three hidden animals are shown by the circles. Did you find any human faces too? There are lots hidden in the picture!

p.38 Hidden Baby
The baby panda is to the right of the mother, in the weeds.

p.39 Lonely Dancers
There is a large face in the centre of the picture.

p.40 Carpet Capers
Both carpets are the same length – check it with a ruler to see!

p.41 Where You Bean?

p.43 Hovering Helicopters
If you concentrate on the circles the red line seems longer, but if you look at the helicopters then the blue line seems longer. In fact, the blue line is the longest of the two.

p.44 Tall and Small
Oddly, the man closest to you is the tallest.

p.46 How Many Angels?
There are two different pairs of angels!

p.51 Chicks in the Nest
You can see either four birds sitting in four nests and one standing on a branch, or four chicks and a mother bird. In all, there are ten birds!

p.52 The Perfect Circle
Yes it is, but the stars around it make it look flattened.

p.54 A Very Odd Place
1. The columns can be rounded or square.
2. The boy's cart is an impossible shape.
3. The fountain is both in front and behind the column.
4. The stairs seem to only go down.
5. The jet of water passes through the stair rail.

p.60 Tiger Tiger
The black and white photograph becomes coloured.

p.65 All Tied Up
The answer is C. The squares are alternately light and dark.

p.67 Box Clever

p.68 The Magic Glass
Just turn the page upside down and the glass looks as if it is no longer on the tray.

p.75 What is it?
We think it might be an elephant standing on its front legs, but you might see something else.

p.77 Guess the Picture
We think this might be two cats drinking from a bowl of milk. What did you come up with?

p.79 Swiss Cross
Did you get it right?

p.81 Hide and Seek
There's a cat hiding in this puzzle.

p.82 Bowling Balls
Both the balls are the same size. Surprised?

p.85 Impossible Objects
None of these objects could exist in real life.

p.87 Wild Child
The hidden boy's face is shown by a circle.

p.88 Fairer Pharaoh
They are both the same shade, but the dark background makes the statue on the left seem lighter.

p.89 Magic Wardrobe
Although the A–B line seems longer, the two lines are actually the same length. Go on, measure them!

p.90 Tricky Triangles
There are 11 triangles in total. Three small white triangles, three small coloured triangles, three large coloured triangles and two hidden triangles, see below.

p.91 Bright Bulb
The yellow colour is the same all over the picture, but the middle circle seems to get brighter as you move it closer and further away from you.

p.93 Leaning Tower Paintings
The painting on the right is the crooked one.

Picture Credits

The authors would like to acknowledge the following sources. Any oversights, omissions or corrections will be updated in future editions of this work.

Page 34: Illusion based on research by J. Flaubert and A. Herbert
Page 51: Photo by Mark Chester
Page 81: The image is based on a computer drawing of Craig S. Kaplan